W9-AYO-554

Collies

Stephanie Finne

Checkerboard
Library

An Imprint of Abdo Publishing
www.abdopublishing.com

Checkerboard
Animal Library
Dogs

www.abdopublishing.com

Published by Abdo Publishing, a division of ABDO, PO Box 398166, Minneapolis, MN 55439.
Copyright © 2015 by Abdo Consulting Group, Inc. International copyrights reserved in all
countries. No part of this book may be reproduced in any form without written permission from
the publisher. Checkerboard Library™ is a trademark and logo of Abdo Publishing.

Printed in the United States of America, North Mankato, Minnesota.
102014
012015

Cover Photo: iStockphoto
Interior Photos: Glow Images pp. 5, 7, 12, 13, 17, 21; iStockphoto pp. 1, 9, 11, 15, 19

Series Coordinator: Tamara L. Britton
Editors: Rochelle Baltzer, Megan M. Gunderson, Bridget O'Brien
Production: Jillian O'Brien

Library of Congress Cataloging-in-Publication Data

Finne, Stephanie, author.
Collies / Stephanie Finne.
    pages cm. -- (Dogs)
Audience: Ages 8-12.
Includes index.
ISBN 978-1-62403-673-6
1. Collie--Juvenile literature. 2. Working dogs--Juvenile literature. I. Title.
SF429.C6F56 2015
636.7374--dc23
                                              2014025406

Contents

The Dog Family

For more than 12,000 years, dogs and humans have lived together. Scientists believe dogs descended from the gray wolf. Like wolves, dogs belong to the family **Canidae.**

Wolves hunted and **scavenged** near villages. Early humans wanted to use these skills to help their own hunt. Humans soon tamed wolves and began to **breed** them. These were the first dogs. They acted as protectors and hunters.

Humans found dogs were good for more than just hunting. So, they developed different types of breeds for different jobs. Today, there are more than 400 breeds. Some dogs are hunters and others are loyal companions. Collies were bred to be herding dogs.

Collies

Little is known about the history of the collie. These strong, responsive dogs have been used for herding in Scotland for centuries. They once herded cows and sheep to market. This is called droving.

In the 1860s, Queen Victoria visited Scotland. She fell in love with the intelligent collie. She returned to London, England, with a few collies. Soon, the **breed**'s popularity spread across England.

As settlers moved to the United States, they brought collies with them to herd livestock. There, Queen Victoria entered one of her collies in the 1878 Westminster Dog Show. The breed's popularity grew. In 1884, the **American Kennel Club (AKC)** formed. The AKC recognized the collie the next year. In 1886, the Collie Club of America formed.

The **AKC** first accepted two types of collies in the same class. These were the rough-coated collie and the smooth-coated collie. Due to the rough-coated collie's popularity, the smooth-coated collie almost disappeared! In the 1950s, the American Smooth Collie Association Inc. was formed to save them. Today, the dogs are shown in separate classes.

Although the breed has two coat varieties, the rough-coated collie is more popular than the smooth-coated collie.

What They're Like

Collies are smart dogs. They are capable of thinking for themselves. But they are very good at taking orders, too. When well trained, these dogs can understand and obey more than 100 commands!

The herding instinct is strong in collies. This includes barking and nipping to keep a group together. Even nonworking pets will try to herd their families. Owners of pet collies must train them not to herd.

Curious collies are easily bored. They want to please their owners. So, they need owners to train them and give them affection. If collies become bored, they may bark a lot or get into trouble.

8

Collies are loyal and nurturing. They bond with all members of the family. They are especially good with children. A devoted collie can be a wonderful addition to your family.

A collie's coat type depended on which animal it herded. The rough collie worked with sheep and the smooth collie worked with cattle.

Coat and Color

Collies come in two types. There are smooth-coated collies and rough-coated collies. Both types have a double coat. The **dense**, thick **undercoat** keeps collies warm.

The smooth-coated collie has a short, hard, and dense outer coat. The rough-coated collie has a longer, straight, hard outer coat.

A smooth-coated collie

Both types of collies have a smooth coat on the face and the front of the legs. Rough-coated collies have a full coat on the mane and the **frill**. Their fur is **feathered** on the back of the legs and the tail.

Collies can be four colors. They can be white or **sable** and white. They can also be tricolor, which is black, tan, and white. Or they can be blue merle. This is mostly a blue-gray with black and white markings.

A rough-coated collie

Size

Collies are medium to large dogs. Females are 22 to 24 inches (56 to 61 cm) tall. They are usually about 50 to 65 pounds (23 to 29 kg). Males are slightly larger. Standing 24 to 26 inches (61 to 66 cm) tall, they weigh 60 to 75 pounds (27 to 34 kg).

A collie has a wedge-shaped head. Its ears are in balance to its head size. When alert, the ears stand erect, with the top fourth of the ear tipping forward.

A rounded **muzzle** tapers to the collie's black nose. The medium-sized, almond-shaped eyes are very dark. Collies have strong bodies. Their straight, muscular legs end in small, oval-shaped paws. The collie's tail is moderately long and twists upward at the tip.

One of the most important parts of judging collies is called expression. This is the overall look of the head.

Care

The expressive collie is known for its athletic abilities. So, a collie needs exercise! Walks twice a day will be good for your collie. Another option is to let it run in a fenced yard.

The smooth-coated collie should be brushed once a week. The rough-coated collie needs grooming every other day. Both types should be brushed more often when **shedding**. Otherwise, their fur can get **matted**.

Brushing isn't the only type of grooming a collie needs. Regular care includes weekly teeth brushing, ear cleaning, and nail trimming. An occasional bath will help keep your dog's fur clean.

Collies require regular checkups with a veterinarian. At its vet visit, the dog will receive **vaccines** and an overall exam. The vet can **spay** or **neuter** dogs that will not be **bred**.

Collies like to be part of a pack. They like to be included in activities and chores. But the most important thing you can give your collie is love.

Grooming a collie is a big responsibility. The coat must be brushed regularly to keep the dog healthy.

Feeding

Adult collies should be fed once or twice a day. Puppies will need to eat several meals a day. To stay healthy, collies need a balanced diet. It must include **protein**. Choose food that is labeled "complete and balanced." This means the food contains all the **nutrients** your dog needs.

There are different types of dog food. Canned foods are moist. But, they spoil quickly and must be stored in a refrigerator. Semimoist foods are softer and do not need to be refrigerated. Dry foods help clean your dog's teeth.

Be sure to discuss types of food and feeding amount options with your vet. A vet can also suggest appropriate treats. Along with food and treats, be sure to always provide your dog with fresh, clean water.

You can start feeding your collie an adult diet when it is nine months old.

Things They Need

Besides food and water, your dog needs a few other things. Start with food and water dishes. Wash these bowls each day to help your dog stay healthy.

You will need combs and brushes to care for your collie's coat. A toothbrush, toothpaste, and nail trimmer are also needed for general care.

Walks are good exercise, so a collar and leash are very important. An identification tag will help your dog be returned if it becomes lost. A vet can insert a **microchip** in your collie, too.

A busy collie is a well-behaved collie! So, provide toys to entertain your dog. Dogs enjoy playing with balls, ropes, and chew toys.

An agility course is also a great way to exercise your collie.

Finally, your collie should have its own bed. You will also want a crate for your new friend. Put a blanket or cushion inside. It will be a soft, comfortable den for your pet.

Puppies

After mating, a female collie is **pregnant** for about 63 days. Having puppies is called whelping. A collie can have two to eight puppies in a **litter**, but the average is five.

Puppies are born blind and deaf. After two weeks, a puppy's eyes open. After four weeks, the puppy can see, hear, and play.

At eight weeks old, a collie is ready to leave its mother. If you want to add a collie to your family, find a **breeder**. A good breeder makes sure the puppy is healthy and has its shots.

Collie puppies learn quickly. Be sure to **socialize** your puppy so it is not scared of strangers. This will help your collie be a loving companion for the next 12 to 14 years.

A puppy first learns about socialization from its littermates.

Glossary

American Kennel Club (AKC) - an organization that studies and promotes interest in purebred dogs.

breed - a group of animals sharing the same ancestors and appearance. A breeder is a person who raises animals. Raising animals is often called breeding them.

Canidae (KAN-uh-dee) - the scientific Latin name for the dog family. Members of this family are called canids. They include wolves, jackals, foxes, coyotes, and domestic dogs.

dense - thick or compact.

feathered - having a fringe of hair.

frill - a ruff of hair or feathers around the neck of an animal.

litter - all of the puppies born at one time to a mother dog.

mat - to form into a tangled mass.

microchip - an electronic circuit placed under an animal's skin. A microchip contains identifying information that can be read by a scanner.

muzzle - an animal's nose and jaws.

neuter (NOO-tuhr) - to remove a male animal's reproductive glands.

nutrient - a substance found in food and used in the body. It promotes growth, maintenance, and repair.

pregnant - having one or more babies growing within the body.

protein - a substance which provides energy to the body and serves as a major class of foods for animals. Foods high in protein include cheese, eggs, fish, meat, and milk.

sable - having black-tipped hairs on a silver, gold, gray, fawn, or brown background.

scavenge - to search through waste for something that can be used.

shed - to cast off hair, feathers, skin, or other coverings or parts by a natural process.

socialize - to adapt an animal to behaving properly around people or other animals in various settings.

spay - to remove a female animal's reproductive organs.

undercoat - short hair or fur partly covered by longer protective fur.

vaccine (vak-SEEN) - a shot given to prevent illness or disease.

Websites

To learn more about Dogs, visit **booklinks.abdopublishing.com**. These links are routinely monitored and updated to provide the most current information available.

Index

A
adoption 20
American Kennel Club 6, 7

B
barking 8
body 12
breeder 20

C
Canidae (family) 4
character 8, 9, 14, 15, 18, 20
coat 7, 10, 11, 14
collar 18
Collie Club of America 6, 7
color 11, 12
crate 18

E
ears 12, 14
England 6
exercise 14
eyes 12, 20

F
food 16, 18

G
grooming 14, 18

H
head 11, 12
health 16, 18, 20
herding 4, 6
history 4, 6

L
leash 18
legs 11, 12
life span 20
litter 20

M
muzzle 12

N
nails 14
neuter 15

P
paws 12
puppies 20

R
reproduction 20

S
Scotland 6
senses 20
shedding 14
size 12
socialization 20
spay 15

T
tail 11, 12
teeth 14, 18
toys 18
training 8

U
United States 6

V
vaccines 15, 20
veterinarian 14, 15, 16, 18
Victoria, Queen 6

W
water 16, 18

24